F.I.G.H.T. C.U.T.

S.T.A.T.

(Securing Techniques And Tactics)

"To win without fighting is best" Sun Tzu

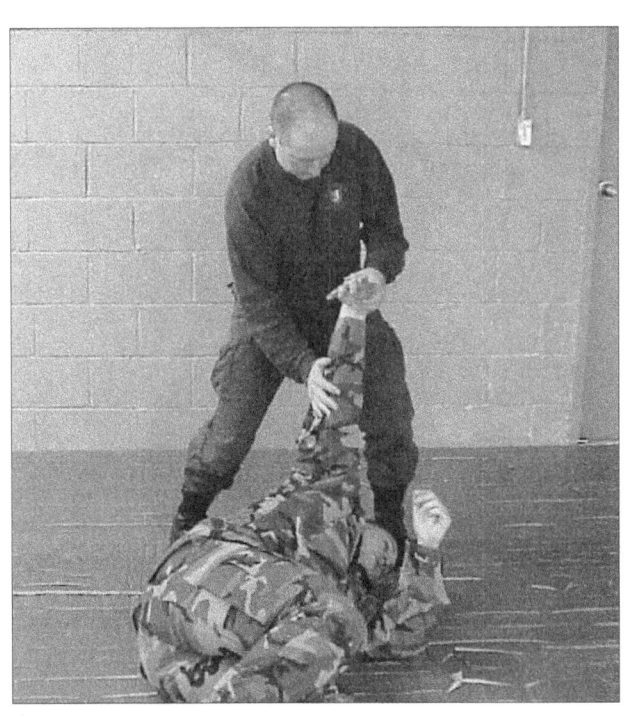

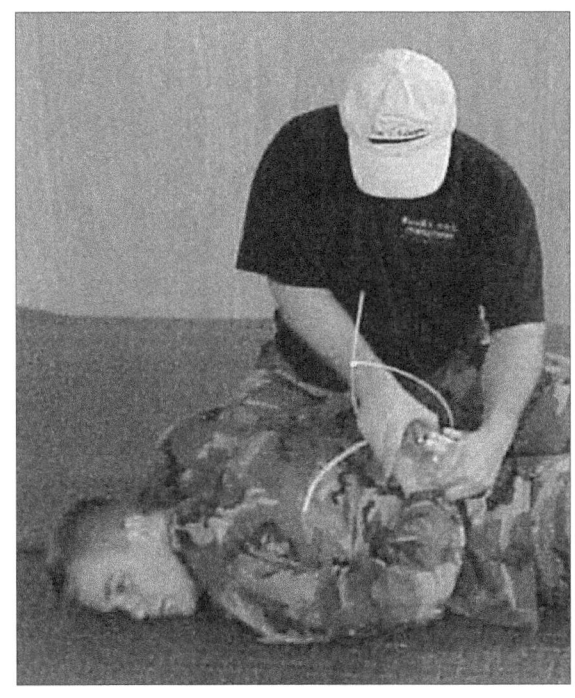

Table of Contents

Contact Information:
David L Sgro Founder F.I.G.H.T. C.U.T./S.T.A.T.
1916 Skibo Rd Suite 210
Fayetteville, NC 28314
(910) 860-1234
e-mail to: dsgro@sktsd.com
www.fightcut.com

What is F.I.G.H.T. C.U.T./STAT?

F.I.G.H.T. C.U.T. (Fully Integrated Grappling and Hitting Techniques, Close Up Techniques) is a Military Combatives Course based on techniques from Japanese Ju-Jitsu, Brazilian Jiu-Jitsu, Karate, and Arnis. There is a tremendous need for CAPOC personnel to train in Combatives, especially in the following areas:

1) Force Continuum from Less force to More Force (Diplomacy to Deadly Force)
2) Blocks and redirections of aggressors attack
3) Joint Locks
4) Arm Bars
5) Come alongs
6) Striking with lethal and non lethal application to insure personnel safety

S.T.A.T. (Securing Techniques And Tactics) is not a combatives course, but rather a Personnel Safety Course, designed and created specifically for the US Soldier where, if the use of force can not be avoided, then the minimal use of force is best. The techniques were selected for their simplicity, effectiveness, and adaptability, to increase combat readiness, personnel safety and survivability. S.T.A.T. teaches how to engage and control an enemy combatant without lethal force. Often this is done with "Live" (unrehearsed) realistic scenarios. Sections of training include full kit. Safety measures are incorporated into the training to sustain high intensity. Students learn quickly with ample time for "skill and drill".

S.T.A.T. training greatly enhances both individual and unit effectiveness. Proficiency in Securing Techniques And Tactics is an essential skill for anyone who finds their self in a hostile environment without a weapon. S.T.A.T. incorporates: minimal use of force, strikes, kicking, joint locks, flex-cuffing, prisoner movement techniques, - with lethal and non-lethal applications, offering a high level of physical endurance and confidence in ones ability to greatly insure personnel safety.

F.I.G.H.T. C.U.T. (Fully Intergraded Grappling and Hitting Techniques & Close Up Techniques)
S.T.A.T. (Securing Techniques And Tactics)
"The rules have changed..." and *"Because the Threat is Real..."*
are Trade Marks, all rights reserved. No part of this publication may be duplicated, reprinted or reproduced in any form without prior written permission of the author.

Copyright 2008 David L. Sgro

About the Founder of F.I.G.H.T. C.U.T.

David L. Sgro first began his studies of the martial arts in 1974 at the age of 13, and has been teaching full time in 1986. He earned his Black Belt in Tang Soo Do (Karate) and Japanese Ju-Jitsu in 1982. He was on TEAM USA in 1986 (England), 1989 (Korea), and 1991 (Argentina), and Coached for TEAM USA in 1999 England, 2001 Greece, 2002 Holland, and 2003 England. He is a 6th Degree Black Belt in Tang Soo Do, a 5th Degree Black Belt in Ju-Jitsu, a Certified Arnis Instructor (Stick/Knife Fighting) and a Blue Belt in Brazilian Jiu-Jitsu.

To create **F.I.G.H.T C.U.T.** he volunteered one year working with the US Army to develop and refine a Combatives Course which would teach the skills needed for Combatives in a simple, direct, and effective manner. **F.I.G.H.T C.U.T.** is now proudly being taught to the US Armed forces. He has literally taught hundreds and hundreds of Soldiers, to include 3rd SFG (A), 7th SFG (A), 1/325, 2/325, 1/504, 2/504, 3/504, 1/505, 3/505, 1/319, 2/319, 3/319, 35th Sig, 82nd Sig, 50th Sig, 51st Sig, 82nd MP, 307th FSB, 407th FSB, 307th ENG, 1/128th FA/MP, 519th MI, 3rd BN POG, USCAPOC, 321 FAR, COSCOM, and VMI (Virginia Military Institute), Special Troops BN, and others.

In addition to running **F.I.G.H.T C.U.T.** he currently owns and operates the Academy of Christian Martial Arts. He attends Manna Church and calls Fayetteville, NC home with his lovely wife (Angela) and children.

"I would first like to personally thank my Lord and Savior Jesus Christ for showing me the real meaning of courage, long suffering, and peace. He is the MAN and the real warrior. Any and all glory, accolades, or anything else that is considered good that comes from this course is given to God, from whom all blessings and good things come from.

David L. Sgro, Combatives Instructor
F.I.G.H.T. C.U.T. Founder

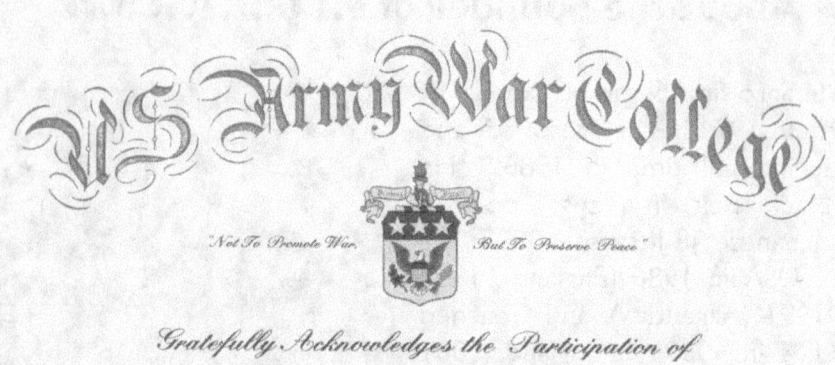

US Army War College

"Not To Promote War, But To Preserve Peace"

Gratefully Acknowledges the Participation of

Mr. David L. Sgro

in the Forty-eighth Annual

National Security Seminar

3 June to 7 June 2002

Carlisle Barracks, Pennsylvania

COLONEL, USA
DEAN OF ACADEMICS

MAJOR GENERAL, USA
COMMANDANT

David L. Sgro, (front row 1st on left) was invited by Col Dick Pedersen (3rd row 4th from right) to attend the US ARMY WAR COLLEGE NATIONAL SECURITY SEMINAR 3-7 June, 2002, Carlisle Barracks, Penn. Col Dick Pedersen is currently serving as the 3rd Brigade Commander, 25th Inf Div (Light).

Brigadier General, Michael Ferriter (82nd ABN ADCO) with David L. Sgro, Founder **F.I.G.H.T. C.U.T. COMBATIVES.** David L. Sgro, and his MTT were responsible for training over 1,100 82nd ABN Paratroopers from July 2004 - July 2005

DEPARTMENT OF THE ARMY
HEADQUARTERS, 1st BATTALION, 325TH AIRBORNE
INFANTRY REGIMENT
FORT BRAGG, NORTH CAROLINA 28310-5100

REPLY TO
ATTENTION OF

AFVC-BA-CDR   31 MAY 2002

MEMORANDUM FOR Whom It May Concern

SUBJECT: Letter of Recommendation for Mr. David Sgro

1. I strongly recommend Mr. David Sgro for Military Unit Combatives Instructor.

2. Mr. David Sgro has been a great asset to our Battalion and has greatly enhanced our combat readiness. His martial arts skills are only surpassed by his instruction ability and his dedication to his country. Mr. Sgro opened up his business and provided his services free of charge on several weekends in order to ensure our paratroopers had the maximum opportunity for combatives training. He personally coached our Battalion combatives team to win the Regimental combatives smoker. This was done of his own accord and is a reflection of his devotion to soldiers. David Sgro moved to the Fayetteville area and opened up his business here to be able to instruct service members. He is a patriot in keeping with the highest attributes of that title.

3. POC for this memorandum is the undersigned at (910) 432-2403.

BRYAN R. OWENS
LTC, IN
Commanding

Instructor David L. Sgro (1st on left Standing). LTC Bryan Owens (Standing 5th from left)
1/325 (AIR) Grappling Trainers 8 Mar 02

"TRAINING THE TRAINERS"
FIGHT CUT FOUNDER David Sgro (2nd row center w/hat) LTC Nantz and Instructor Ray Simpson (next to LTC Nantz) with 1/325 INF (ABN) MOUT Combatives training 13 Apr 04

 1-325TH AIRBORNE INFANTRY REGIMENT

RED FALCONS

CERTIFICATE OF APPRECIATION

~ AWARDED TO ~

David L. Sgro

23 April 2004

For your continued commitment to maintain the combat readiness of the
1st Battalion, 325th Airborne Infantry Regiment. Your personal
commitment and intense training programs have contributed immensely
to the battalions combatives program and made this battalion more
combat ready.

AIRBORNE, ALL THE WAY

LET'S GO!

TITO ORTIZTORRES
CSM, USA
Command Sergeant Major

ERIC W. NANTZ
LTC, IN
Commanding

9

F.I.G.H.T. C.U.T. taught to the 82nd MP Co
1 Oct 04

"While working law enforcement duty on Fort Bragg my partner and I were called to the Yadkin access control point for a heroin hit on the itemizer (a machine that detects the scent of drugs and drug paraphernalia). Upon arrival we made contact with the suspect who stated that he was driving a friends vehicle and did not have anything on him. I notified him of the situation and the fact that I would need to search him as well as the vehicle. He complained but complied when asked to remove all items from his pockets. When asked to remove his BDU top he complied after having to be told a second time. When asked to turn and face away from me placing his hands on top of his head and interlocking his fingers he refused. I told the subject two more times and he refused. I told the subject that I was only going to tell him one more time and repeated my original request. As soon as he said "no" I placed my right leg behind both of his and pushed with my right arm on his shoulder moving him towards the ground. We wrestled a little bit and while I placed his left arm in an arm bar my partner grabbed his right arm and we finished taking him to the ground. When the subject hit the ground I placed him in a wrist lock with is left arm between my legs, right knee on his left shoulder blade, and left knee on the back of his neck. I then placed the subject in hand irons. The techniques I learned and then implemented from the F.I.G.H.T. C.U.T. class enabled me to take this particular subject to the ground quickly, and enabled me to catch my breath while I had him in the wristlock."

SGT John A. Freeland
82nd MP Co.
82nd ABN DIV

Definition of terms:

Use Of Force In Defense Of Person.
A person is justified in the use of force against another when and to the extent that he reasonably believes that such conduct is necessary to defend himself or another against such other's imminent use of unlawful force. However, he is justified in the use of force which is intended or likely to cause death or great bodily harm **only if he reasonably believes that such force is necessary to prevent imminent death or great bodily harm to himself or another.**

ASSAULT: To intentionally place someone in imminent fear of battery, or to threaten someone while having the apparent ability to carry that threat out.

BATTERY: Any form of intentional, non-consensual bodily contact that a reasonable person would consider harmful or offensive.

OVERVIEW OF USE OF FORCE

Soldiers should be familiar with the following legal terms. These terms appear in state laws that defined an soldier's legal authority for the use of force. This terminology may be different from state to state, however, the legal concepts are the same.

Force:

1) Physical Force: the application of enough force to overcome resistance, but not amounting to deadly physical force.

2) Deadly Physical Force: the application of enough force to cause death or serious physical injury.

3) Serious Physical Injury: *Serious or protracted disfigurement, amputation, or, loss or impairment of the use of a bodily function or organ.*

Non-Lethal Weapon:

Includes the ASP expandable baton and Oleoresin Capsicum (OC) Spray.

Justified Use of Force:

The use of force is justified when it is authorized by law (ROE), when it is necessary, reasonable, and absent recklessness. Soldiers are not relieved of liability for the reckless or excessive use of force.

Levels of Resistance

Listed below are descriptions of the levels of resistance a person might offer when being arrested. The levels are listed from least resistance to greatest resistance.

Cooperative: the person willingly complies with the soldier's directions while the soldier is attempting to flex cuff him. The person offers no resistance.

Intimidation: this is the first level of resistance. Intimidation, if left unchecked, creates a possibility of resistance. Resistance may take several different forms to include:
1) Verbal taunting
2) Attempts to distract the Solider
3) Threats of injury (See "assault and battery")
4) Making racial slurs
5) Using profanity or vulgarity of a nature that would tend to inflame another person.

Constructive Resistance:
1) Walking away from a Soldiers command
2) Refusing to comply with other attempts by the Soldier to gain control of the situation.
3) Physical attempts to pull or jerk away from the Solider are at this level.
However, the person does not direct physical force towards the soldier.

Physical Resistance: this includes:
1) Grabbing
2) Pushing
3) Punching
4) Kicking
5) Biting
6) Throwing objects at the Soldier.
The person has committed a battery on the Soldier.

Deadly Resistance: the highest level of resistance and includes the person's demonstrated intentions to seriously injure the soldier or render him/her unconscious or incapable of self-protection. Such actions as attempts to grab the officer's baton, firearm, OC Spray, high-velocity strikes and blows at the soldier's head, throat, or vital organs, and any action that if successfully completed would have a high probability of causing serious lasting or permanent injury or death.

Levels of Force In Response to Resistance

Listed below are the levels of force soldiers may apply in response to the level of resistance offered. The levels are listed from the least amount of force to the greatest amount of force applied.

Compliance Control: this includes all lawful commands as well as verbal orders. The purpose is to establish physical control of the person to accomplish a lawful frisk, an arrest, handcuffing, a search, an investigative detention, or a custodial procedure.

Physical Control: this includes physically touching, grabbing, knocking off balance, or holding the person. The purpose is to accomplish a lawful frisk, an arrest, handcuffing, search, an investigative detention or a custodial procedure.

Persuasive Tactics and Compliance Commands: included is the use of pressure points, pain compliance holds, and physical takedowns. The purpose is to overcome and control the person's physical resistance. There is no expectation that the application of force at this level will cause lasting, serious, or permanent injury, or death.

Non-Lethal Tactics and Weapons: this includes deliberate use of any physical skills, tactics or impact weapons, to defend the soldier against a person's physical assault. The purpose is to overcome and stop physical resistance while minimizing the risk of serious injury, or death.

Survival Tactics: a soldier may use any tactic, including lethal force, to prevent or mitigate what the soldier reasonably believes to be the imminent threat of deadly assault.

The figure below represents the Use of Force Continuum. The figure illustrates the relationship between the level of resistance offered by a person and the commensurate level of force applied by the soldier.

Level of Resistance from Offender	Level of Force Applied by Solider	Tactic Applied By Soldier
1) Cooperative	Compliance Control	Verbal Communication
2) Intimidation	Physical Control	Verbal Communication and Minimal Physical Force
3) Constructive Resistance	Persuasive Tactics and Compliance Commands	Pressure Points, Pain, Compliance Holds, Physical Takedowns, Handcuffing
4) Physical Resistance	Non-Lethal Tactics and Weapons	Impact Weapons and OC Spray, Striking, Kicking, Handcuffing
5) Deadly Resistance	Survival Tactics	Application of Deadly Force

STAT Help Sheet Task 1-14

Task 1: C.AT (Control Axis Technique)
1) Inside Parry
2) Outside parry
3) CAT Clinch 1 (Natural Response)
4) CAT Clinch 2 (Natural Response)

Task 2: Combat Roll (5 Steps)
1) Combat Stance
2) Prepare
3) Push off
4) Combat Roll
5) Slap Out

Task 3: Standard Wrist Lock (3 Steps)
1) Contact 1st Gear 90 Degrees
2) Capture 2nd Gear 45 Degrees
3) Control 3rd Gear Cut 45 Degrees

Task 4: Turn Over (3 Steps)
1) 1st Gear
2) Lock Elbow
3) Turn Over

Task 5: Chicken Wing (5 Steps)
1) Bend Elbow
2) Drop Knee
3) Secure Elbow
4) Controlling Knee
5) 1st Gear

Task 6: Flexcuffing & Search (8 Steps)
1) 1st Cuff On
2) Grab Fingers
3) Drag Hand
4) Pull Hand & Finish
5) Separate Legs
6) Grab Elbow & Knee
7) Lift & Rest
8) Search

Task 7: Standing up the PUC (4 Steps)
1) Place Hands
2) Turn Over
3) Bend Knee
4) Stand Up

Task 8: SLAB & CAB (4 Steps)
1) Control Wrist
2) Lock Elbow
3) Weld the Hip
4) Take Down

Task 9: Rear Chicken Wing & Take Down (6 Steps)
1) Pour Water
2) Push & Pull
3) Chicken Wing
4) Place Foot
5) Push Knee
6) Chicken Wing

Task 10: Binding Chain (3 Steps)
1) Grab Wrist
2) Lock Elbow
3) Lift & Lock

Task 11: Gooseneck Comealong (3 Steps)
1) Wrist/Elbow
2) Secure Elbow
3) Gooseneck

Task 12 Figure Turn Over (5 Steps)
1) 1st Gear
2) Grab Your Wrist
3) Takedown
4) Half Track
5) Figure 4

Task 13: Alex Entry (Throat Punch) (6 Steps)
1) Raise Weapon
2) Strike
3) Aim
4) Throat Punch
5) Stomp Weapon
6) 3 Times

Task 14: Striking (5 Steps)
1) Palm Heel
2) Elbow (Cross, Reverse, Upward, Downward, Slashing)
3) Knee (Front, Round)
4) Front Kick
5) Round Kick

Task 1 C.A.T. (Controlling Axis Techniques)

An "**Inside Parry**" is when the hand (demonstrated above with the right hand) makes an inside blocking motion (from the center of the body to the outside)

An "**Outside Parry**" is when the hand (demonstrated above with the left hand) makes an outside blocking motion (from the outside of the body to the inside)

(Above Left) "Talking Position" Hands are up in a potential defensive position (Non aggressive)

1) Inside Parry: Right hand makes an inside (from the center of the body) to outside parry motion

2) Grab the opponents wrist with your right hand and prepare to upset his balance with your left

3) Upset his balance by pushing his shoulder (Axis B) with your left hand

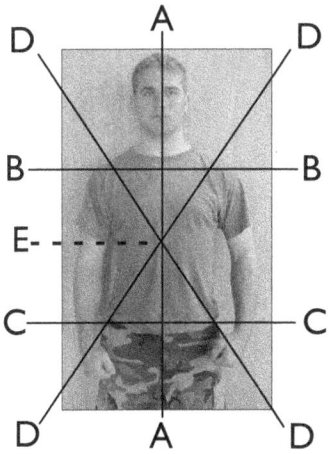

A) Spine Axis
B) Shoulder Axis
C) Hip Axis
D) Cross Should/Hip Line
E) Solar Plexus

Note:
To upset the opponents balance:
Upset 1 axis to upset balance
Upset 2 axis for a minor throw.
Upset 3 axis for a major throw.

Task 2 Combat Roll (5 Steps)

1) **"COMBAT STANCE"** Basic combat fighting stance

2) **"PREPARE"** The soldier places his hand on the ground to prepare for his forward roll.

3) **"PUSH OFF"** The soldier pushes off transferring the weight from his hand to his arm and begins his forward roll.

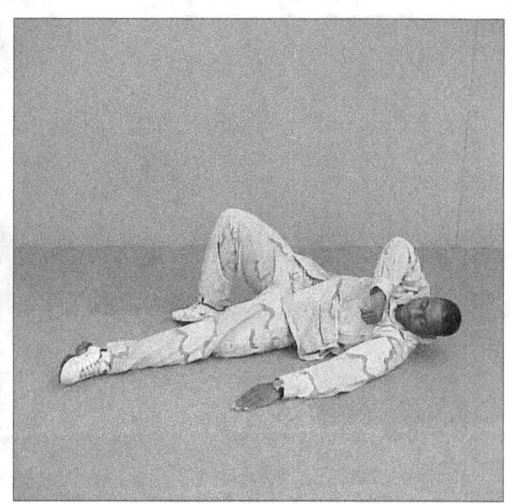

4) **"COMBAT ROLL"** The soldier rolls onto his shoulder and upper back.

5) **"SLAP OUT"** The soldier completes the roll by slapping the map with his left arm and leg, thereby transferring his weight. He lands on the sole of his right foot.

5 steps to "Combat Roll"
1) Combat Stance
2) Prepare
3) Push off
4) Combat Roll
5) Slap out

Notes:

Task 3 "Standard Wrist Lock" (3 steps)

"CONTACT" (To hit or grab)

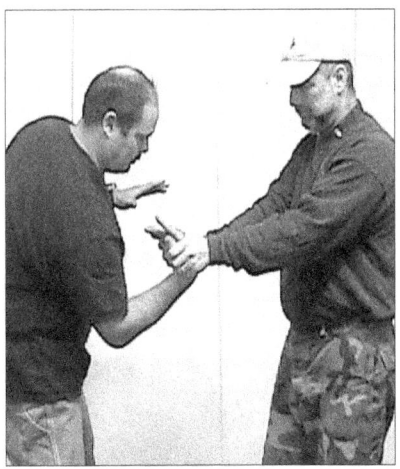

1) **"1st Gear"** Get a firm grip with as much of your hands as possible

(Close up) Bend the opponents wrist to **1st Gear, a 90 degree angle**

"CAPTURE" (To pull)

2) **"2nd Gear"** Pull the opponents hand and twist the hand to **2nd gear, a 45 degree angle**

"CONTROL" (Pain)

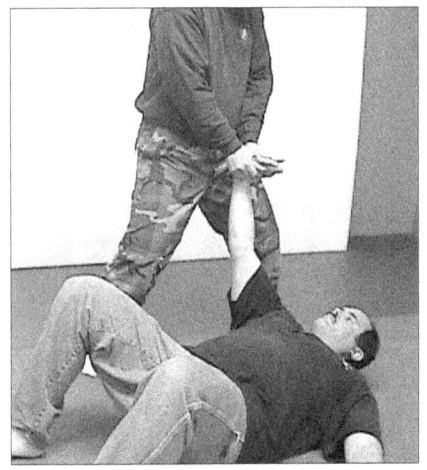

3) **"3rd Gear"** Bend the opponents wrist to **3rd gear, a "Cut 45 degree angle"** and step back with your left foot to create the **"LZ"**

3 steps to "Standard Wrist Lock"
1) Contact 1st Gear
2) Capture 2nd Gear
3) Control 3rd Gear

Note:
3 reasons to teach 1st Gear:
1) To stretch your partners wrist
2) To develop a proper grip
3) To teach an important position which will be used later

3 reasons to keep your back straight in the finish position (bending knees, not back)
1) When you bend your body forward you loose situation awareness
2) When wearing a full kit, leaning forward puts a strain on your lower back
3) By leaning forward, you increase your chances of being rolled by your opponent

Notes:

Task 4: "Turn over" from wrist lock (3 steps)

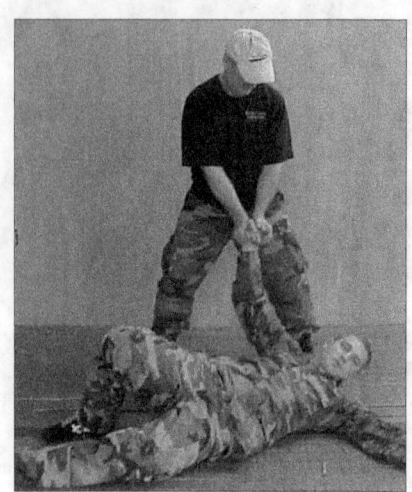 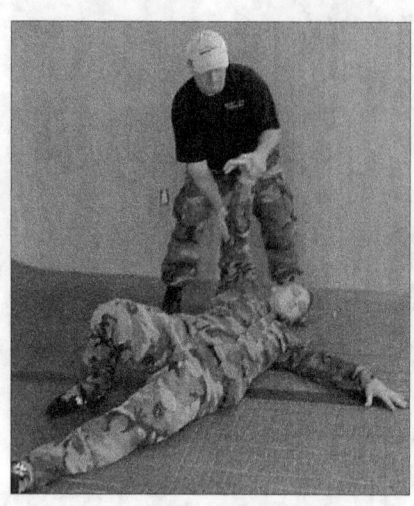 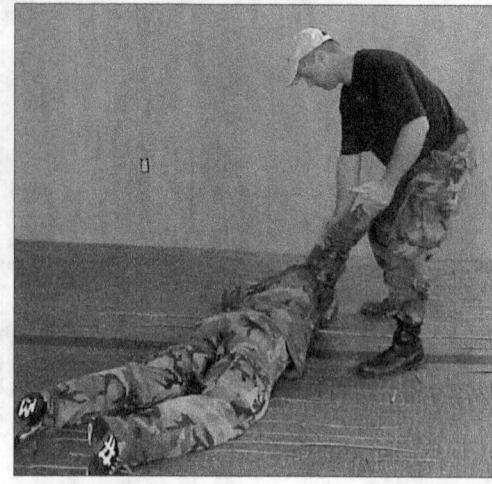

1) **"1st Gear"** Put the opponents wrist in **1st Gear, a 90 degree angle**

2) **"Lock Elbow"** Place your right hand on the opponents elbow

3) **"Turn Over"** Turn the opponent over onto his stomach.

3 steps to "Chicken Wing"
1) 1st Gear
2) Lock Elbow
3) Turn Over

Notes:

Task 5: "Chicken Wing" (5 steps)

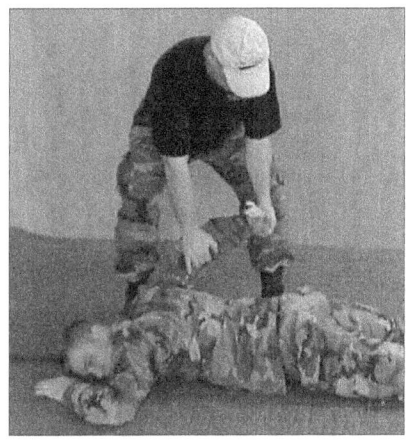

1) **"Bend Elbow"** Bend the opponents arm to **90 degrees**

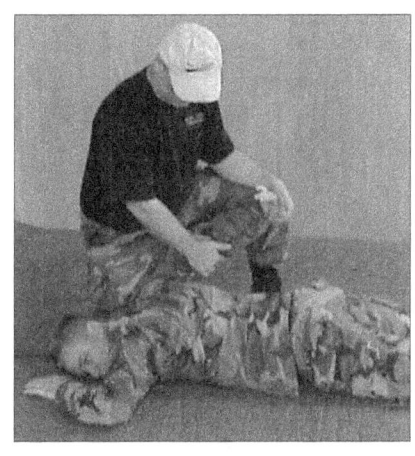

2) **"Drop Knee"** Drop your right knee next to the opponents head

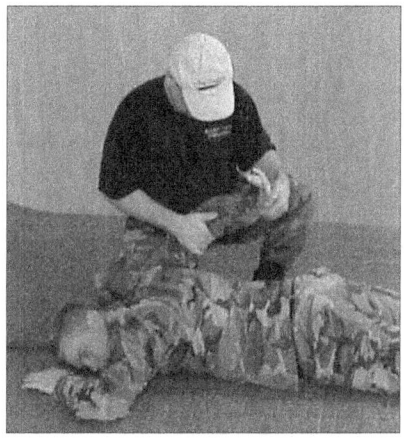

3) **"Elbow to Naval"** Place the opponents elbow in your abdomen

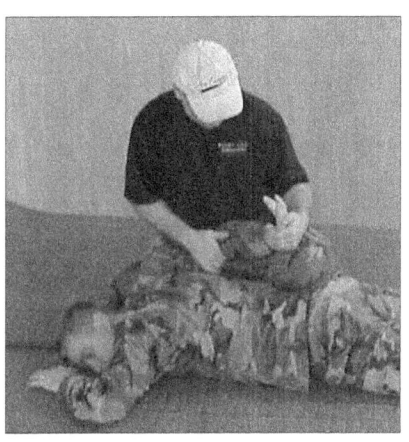

4) **"Controlling Knee"** Press your left knee against the back

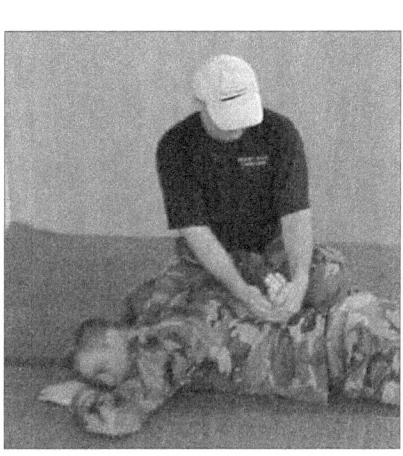

5) "**1st Gear**" Apply **1st Gear** to control his wrist to flex cuff

5 steps to "Chicken Wing"
1) Bend Elbow
2) Drop Knee
3) Elbow to Naval
4) Controlling Knee
5) 1st Gear

Notes:

Task 6 Flexcuffing & Search (8 Steps)

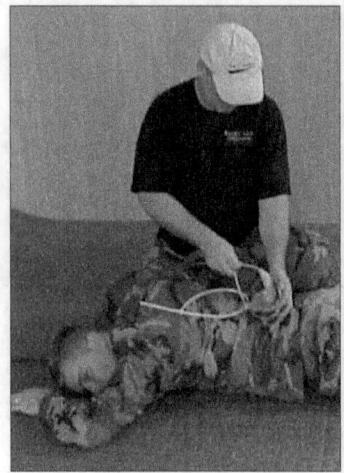  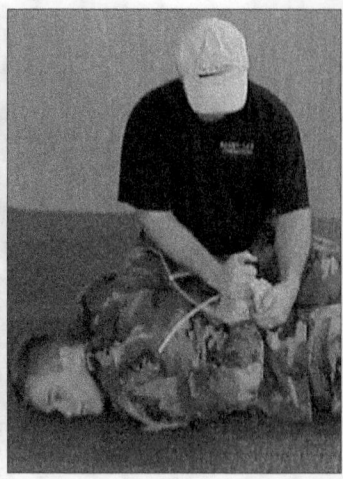 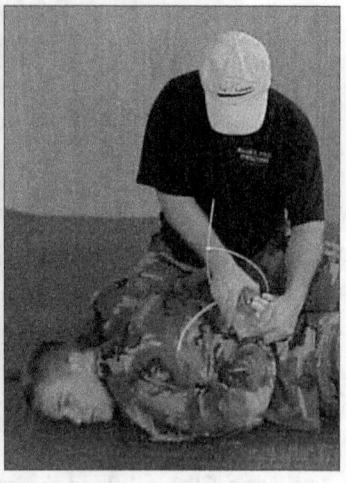

1) **"1st Cuff On"** First place the flex cuff over the thumb then the pinky, then tighten the flex cuff

2) **"Grab Fingers"** Grab the opponents last two fingers

3 **"Drag Hand"** Drag the opponents hand to his back

4) **"Pull Hand & Finish"** Grab his pinky and thumb, squeeze his hand closed, pull his hand through the cuff and finish

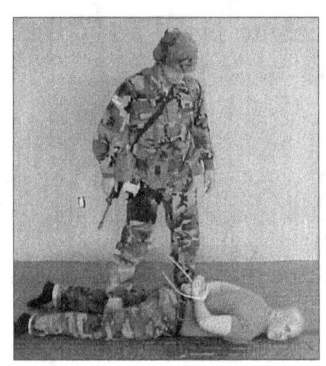 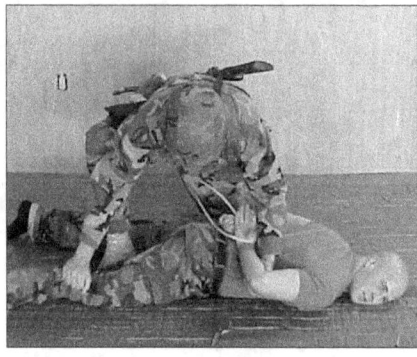  

5) **"Separate Legs"** Place your foot between his legs. If he gets aggressive you can use your knee to control him.

2) **"Grab Elbow & Knee"** Grab the opponents elbow & knee

3 **"Lift & Rest"** Lift the opponents up and rest his leg on your knee

4) **"Search"** Start your search at the opponents ankle and work up his side, then move to the other side

8 steps to "Flexcuffing & Search"
1) 1st Cuff On
2) Grab Fingers
3) Drag Hand
4) Pull Hand & Finish
5) Separate Legs
6) Grab Elbow & Knee
7) Lift & Rest
8) Search

Notes:

Task 7 Standing the PUC up (4 Steps)

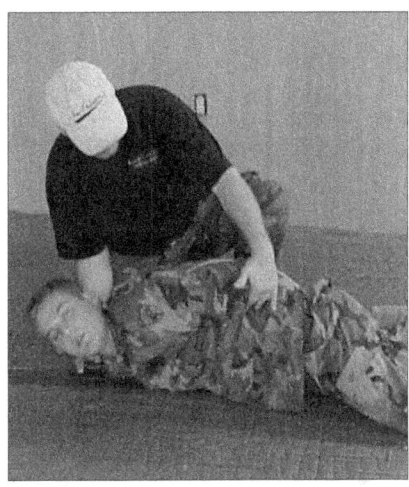

1) **"Place Hands"** Place your right hand (Controlling hand) on the jaw line, left hand (Working hand) on the elbow

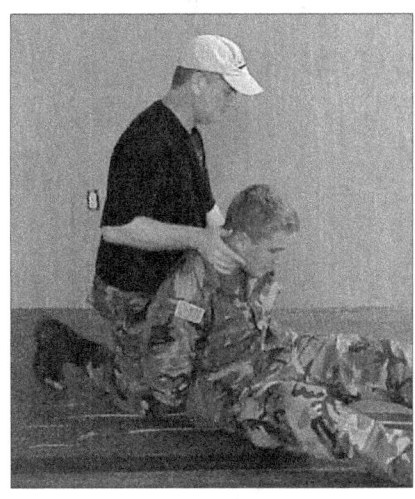

2) **"Turn Over"** Turn him over and sit him up

(Viewing Angle turned forward for better viewing)

3) **"Bend Knee"** Bend the opponents left knee, (keep your hand on his jawline)

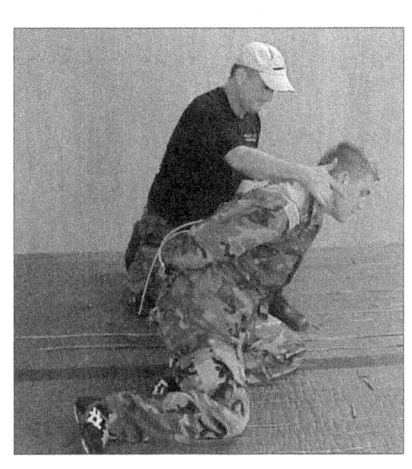

4) **"Stand Up"** Return your left hand to his elbow, turn him onto his left knee and stand him up

Finish Position

4 steps to "Standing Up the PUC"
1) Place Hands
2) Turn Over
3) Bend Knee
4) Stand Up

Notes:

Task 8 SLAB: Arm Bar (4 Steps)
SLAB: Straight Line Arm Bar & CAB: Circular Arm Bar

"CONTACT" (To hit or grab)

(Above Left) "Talking Position" Hands are up in a potential defensive position (Non aggressive approach)

1) **"Control Wrist"** Right hand makes an inside (from the center of the body) to outside parry motion

2) **"Lock Elbow"** Left hand strikes the back of the elbow on the opponent

"CAPTURE" (To pull)   "CONTROL" (To cause pain)

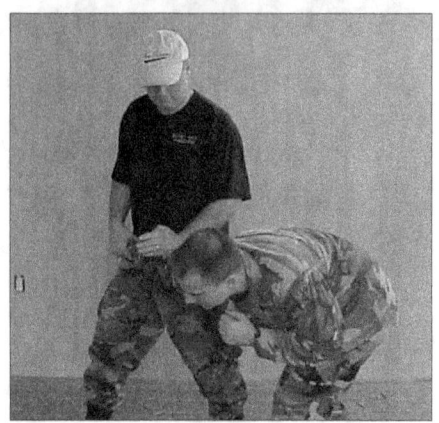

3) **"Weld the hip"**, Drive the opponents arm forward with your left hand

4) **"Take Down"** Continue the motion until the he is on the ground

...to flex cuff transfer his arm from your right hand to your left hand

and get "1st Gear" on your opponents wrist. Now proceed to the "Chicken Wing" and then flex cuffing

4 steps to "SLAB & CAB"
1) Control Wrist
2) Lock Elbow
3) Weld the Hip
4) Take Down

Note: To make a CAB just use circular footwork at you take the opponent to the ground

Notes:

Task 9 Rear Chicken Wing & Take Down (6 Steps)

"CONTACT"

"CAPTURE"

"CONTROL"

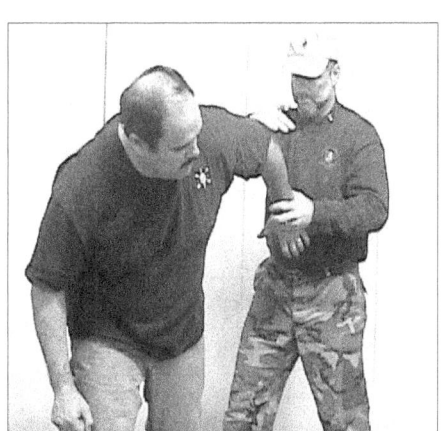

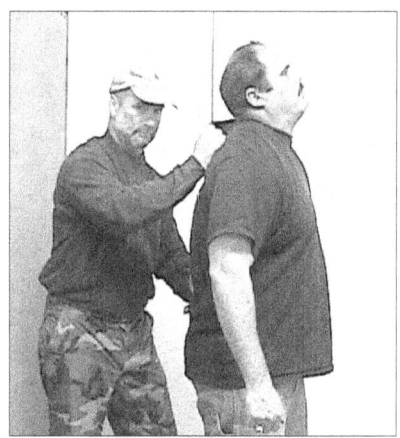

1) **"Pour Water"** Grab the opponents hand

2) **"Push & Pull"** Push the elbow and pull the wrist (If the opponent pulls his arm you can use his force against him.)

3) **"Chicken Wing"**

6 steps to "Rear Chicken Wing & Take Down
1) Pour Water
2) Push & Pull
3) Chicken Wing
4) Place Foot
5) Push Knee
6) Chicken Wing

Notes:

"CONTACT"

"CAPTURE"

"CONTROL"

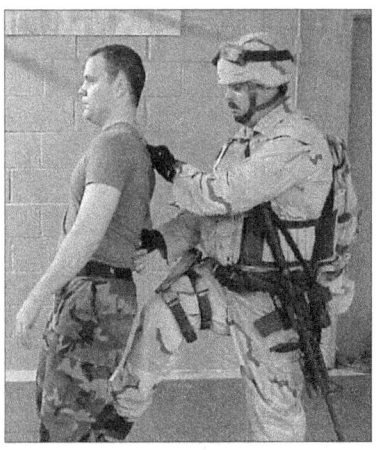

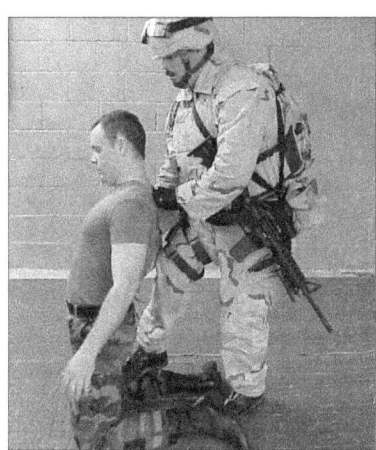

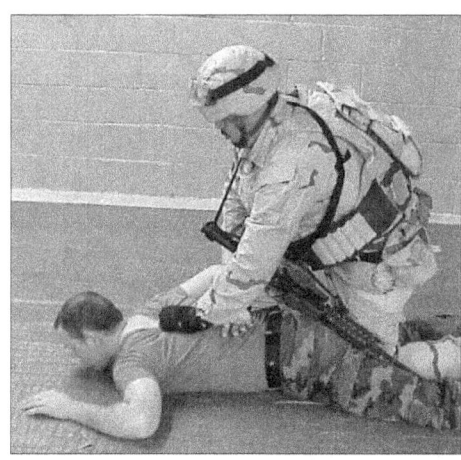

4) **"Place Foot"** Put your foot behind his right knee

5) **"Push Knee"** Drive him to the ground with your foot

6) **"Chicken Wing"** Move to a flex cuffing position (either rear or side)

Task 10 Binding Chain (3 Steps)

"CONTACT"
(To hit or grab)

"CAPTURE"
(To pull)

"CONTROL"
(To cause pain)

(1) **"Grab Wrist"** Grab your opponents wrist with your right hand

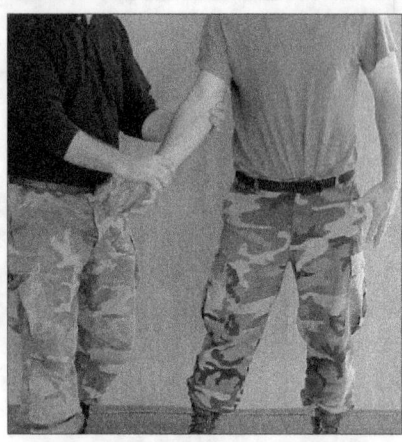

2) **"Lock Elbow"** Secure his elbow with your left hand and pull his right hand towards your body as your tork his wrist

3) **"Lift & Lock"** Lift up your opponents arm to apply the Arm Bar Comealong. (Note: Heels are off the floor as the pain is applied)

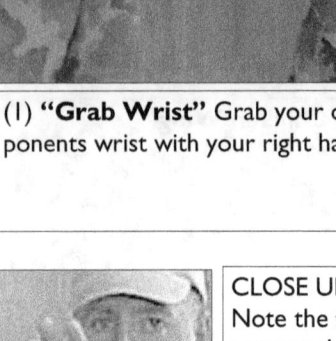

CLOSE UP: Note the thumb secures the lock by being placed on the crease line of the opponents wrist

3 steps to "Binding Chain"
1) Grab Wrist
2) Lock Elbow
3) Lift & Lock

3 steps to "Gooseneck Comealong"
1) Wrist/Elbow
2) Secure Elbow
3) Gooseneck

Task 11 Gooseneck Comealong (3 Steps)

"CONTACT"
(To hit or grab)

"CAPTURE"
(To pull)

"CONTROL"
(To cause pain)

1) **"Wrist/Elbow"** Grab your opponents wrist with your right hand, and secure the inside of his elbow with your left hand

2) **"Secure Elbow"** Secure your opponents elbow against your Body Armor with your left hand and bend his wrist to "**1st Gear**"

3) **"Gooseneck"** Move your hand from your opponents elbow to hand. Apply pressure to secure the Gooseneck Comealong.

Task 12 Figure 4 Chicken Wing (5 Steps)

"CONTACT" (To hit or grab)

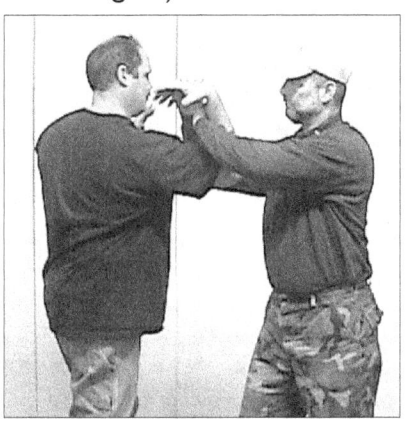

1) **"1st Gear"** Bend the opponents wrist to **1st Gear**

2) **"Grab Your Wrist"** Grab your own wrist with your other hand

"CAPTURE" (To pull)

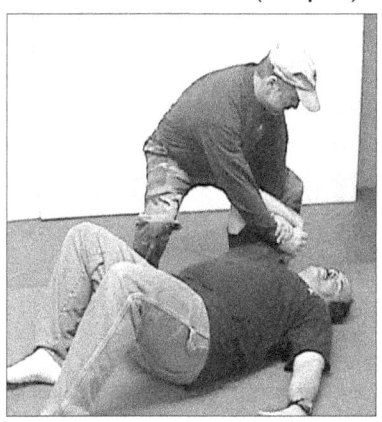

3) **"Takedown"** Take the opponent down by stepping with your left foot creating an **LZ**

"CONTROL" (To cause pain)

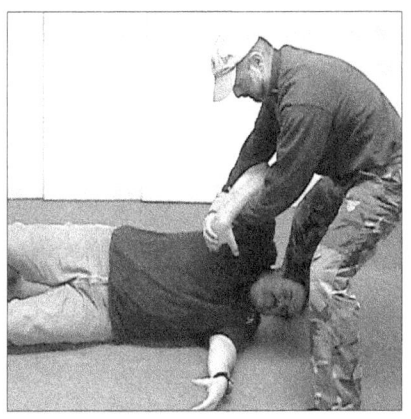

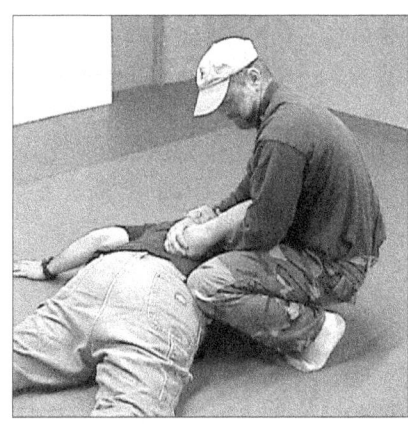

4) **"Half Track"** Move around the opponents head while maintaining the Figure 4 Chicken wing

5) **"Figure 4"** Apply the Chicken wing.

5 steps to "Figure 4 Chicken wing"
1) 1st Gear
2) Grab Your Wrist
3) Takedown
4) Half Track
5) Figure 4

Notes:

Task 13 Alex Entry

Task: Conduct proper techniques to employ the ALEX ENTRY. (Utilize the M4 or SAW itself as a weapon against an opponent armed with an M4).

Condition: Given an Attacker/Soldier who is wearing full combat gear or modified uniforms during good or limited visibility.

Standard: The Soldier properly utilizes the ALEX ENTRY to defend against an opponent armed with a AK 47.

NOTE: The Alex Entry is named after it's originator, Alex Mordine (For more info on Alex Mordine visit www.gracieacademy.com then click on "Gracie Japan"). Alex was visiting Ft Bragg on business in June 2001. He took a "wrong" turn on N. Reilly Rd and happened across my school, "Academy of Christian Martial Arts". As he was a Christian himself he wanted to visit "the new school on Reilly Rd". The day he visited was also the very first time the FIGHT CUT 20 HOUR Combatives course was being taught to SF (Special Forces). Alex is also a Combatives instructor. He reviewed the POI for the course and said it was a great course. The only area of concern was the M4 techniques (the POI was going to teach the techniques taught in ARMY Basic Training.) Alex explained those techniques were derived from the M16 (which were derived from the M1 Grand, trench warfare) but the techniques would not work with the M4 because of three reasons:

1) Most Soldiers now wear a sling (Making a "Butt Stroke" obsolete

2) The collapsible stock eliminates the "Butt Stroke" obsolete because there is no weight in the stock.

3) Since we are no longer fighting in a "Trench warfare" environment now, but rather an Urban Environment with a "Stack" of Soldiers when we hit someone with the "Butt Stroke" we take our barrel off the target and "flag" our fellow Soldiers

Not only did this argument make sense, but the technique he demonstrated made better sense and were incorporated in, on the spot. When asked what he called the technique he said he didn't have a name for it, so they were named the "ALEX ENTRY" to give credit to it's originator: Alex Mordine, and there you have "the rest of the story".

Task 13 The Alex Entry M4 vs. AK 47 (6 Steps)

The Solider is armed with an M4 and the Opponent is armed with an AK47

1) **"Raise Weapon"** As the Opponent raises his AK 47 the Solider side steps and raises his M4

2) **"Strike"** The Solider strikes down against the Opponents wrist, causing him to drop his AK 47

3) **"Aim"** The Solider prepares to thrust the barrel of the M4 into the Opponents throat.

4) **"Throat Punch"** The Solider drives the barrel into the Opponents throat with a "throat punch".

5) **"Stomp Weapon"** The Solider secures the AK 47 as he prepares to drive the barrel into the Opponents throat.

6) **"3 times"** The Solider drives the his M4 into the opponents throat. (Repeat 3 times in training) Then secure the opponents weapon

6 steps to "Alex Entry Throat Punch"
1) Raise Weapon
2) Strike
3) Aim
4) Throat Punch
5) Stomp Weapon
6) 3 Times

Notes:

27

Task 14 Striking "Palm Heel & Elbow"

1) Combat Stance

2) **"Palm Heel"** Throw a Palm Heel Strike to the opponents Face. Drive in with your hip while pushing forward onto the ball of your back foot.

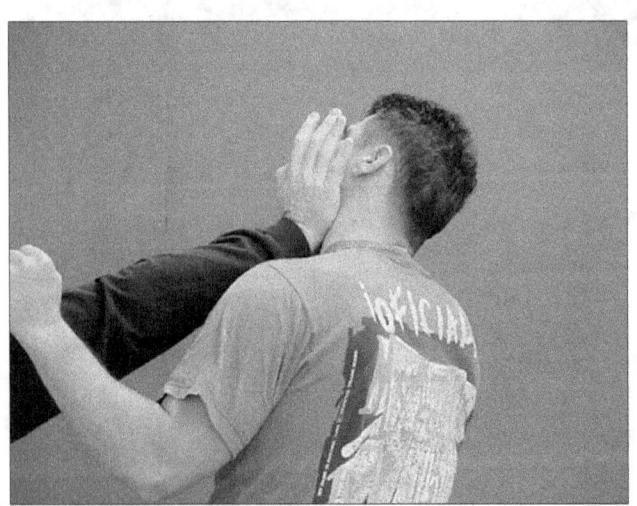

2a) Close up of Palm Heel Strike

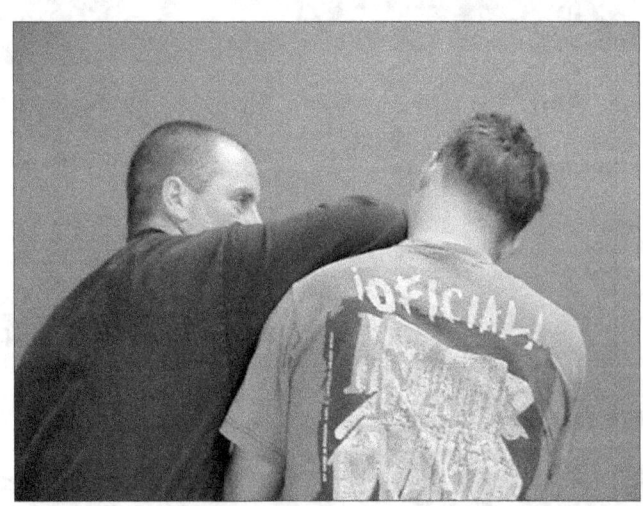

3) **"Elbow"** Throw an elbow Strike to the opponents face/temple./throat. Drive in with your hip during the attack

Task 14 "Front Kick"

1) Combat Stance

1) Raise your knee to prepare for a front kick

2) Front Kick: Targets include knee, groin, and solar plexus. Drive forward with your hips, keep your back foot flat

3) Retract your kicking leg to prevent the opponent from grabbing your leg.

Task 14 "Round Kick"

1) Combat Stance

1) Raise your knee to prepare for a round kick

2) Round Kick: Targets include knee, groin, and solar plexus. Drive forward with your hips, keep your back foot flat.

2a) The Round Kick from the reverse angle.

Task 14 Strikes against a grab on the M4 (4 Steps)

The opponent grabs your M4 with a "Two Hand Grab"

1) Strike the opponents chin or face with a right palm heel.

2) The Soldier strikes the Opponents jaw with a right elbow.

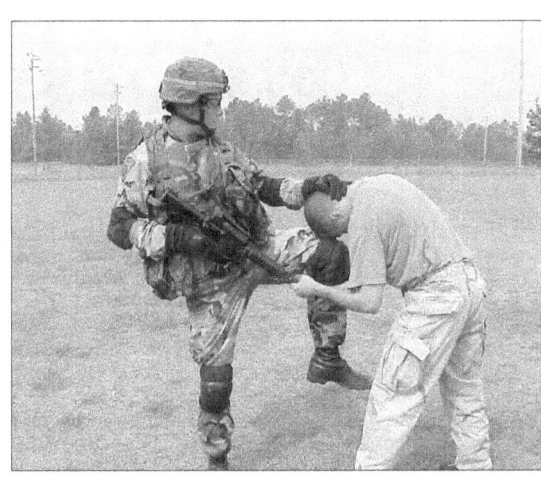

3) The Soldier kicks the Opponents face (or groin) with a knee kick

4) and delivers a front kick to the Opponents stomach or groin.

Be it known that

Has successfully completed the
STAT
(SECURING TECHNIQUES AND TACTICS)
20 HOUR
PERSONNEL SAFETY COURSE

At this institution
On this the ___ Day of ___ 2008

Given at the
F.I.G.H.T. C.U.T.
COMBATIVES ACADEMY
FAYETTEVILLE, N.C.

DAVID L. SGRO
FOUNDER F.I.G.H.T. C.U.T./S.T.A.T.